The View From the 86th Floor

The Empire State Building and New York City

John Tauranac

Contents

The Empire State Building, 2

The Views
North Views, 4–11
North Views Up Close, 12–17
Northeast Views, 18–25
East Views, 26–31
Southeast Views, 32–37
South Views, 38–47
South Views Up Close, 48–53
Southwest Views, 54–59
West Views, 60–67
Northwest Views, 68–75
Looking Down, 76–79

Maps
Metropolitan New York, Inside Front Cover
Manhattan South from the Empire State Building, 80
Manhattan North from the Empire State Building, Inside Back Cover

Editor: Susan Eddy
Principal Photographer: Petra Liebetanz
Cover and 1997 Views: Sari Goodfriend
Other photographs courtesy of The Empire State Building Company LLC,
the Library of Congress, and the New York City Municipal Archives
Post card of The Singer Building courtesy of Ellen Stern
Designer: Peter Joseph
Printer: C & C Offset Printing, Hong Kong

Visit Our Web Site: tauranac.com
Fax: 212-222-7731

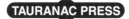

The Empire State Building

The 86th floor of the Empire State Building offers a panorama of New York City and the entire metropolitan region that is world famous. There is only one problem with it.

Whether you are a native or a visitor, you might not know what you are looking at when you gaze out upon this vast metropolis. If you ask, the odds are pretty good you will be given misleading information by someone who is well-meaning but ill-informed, or you might simply be met by a chorus of "I don't knows."

This series of views sets out to solve the problem. Following each full-color picture is exactly the same view in black and white, with all the major buildings, landmarks and geography identified. First you see the view in color, then you are told what you are looking at in black and white. Following the major views are night views of the same area and, in some instances, historic photographs so that you can see the changing cityscape.

The views follow the eight compass points, and you should remember this: North to a New Yorker is straight up Fifth Avenue, when in fact true north is more the angle created by Broadway at 34th Street. The Empire State Building's own directional markers and our compass points all follow the same skewed perspective. We ask for your willing suspension of disbelief.

The book is arranged in sequence as if you are walking clockwise around the building, starting with the view north. You have close-up views both north and south so that you can see some of the details in Midtown and the Financial District. And the last set of photographs shows four views that are looking down rather than out. When you do look down, by the way, don't be surprised if you cannot make out the streets or avenues flanking the Empire State Building. The building itself blocks the views.

If you had looked south from the 86th floor of the Empire State Building any time from the early 1970s until September 11, 2001, you would have seen the twin towers of the World Trade Center rising 1,350 feet into the sky. Upon their completion, the towers reigned as the world's tallest buildings, but in less time than it takes to watch an action-adventure movie, the towers were reduced to ashes.

Until the World Trade Center tragedy, the city had over 140 buildings that were 500 feet tall or taller (152 meters), thirteen buildings at 750 feet tall or taller (227 meters), and four that were taller than 1,000 feet (303 meters). Buildings that loom large in other cities would seldom warrant a second glance in New York City.

The loss of the towers makes the Empire State Building that much more important. Yes, it is once again the city's tallest building, but its importance lies deeper than that. The Empire State Building is peerless. It has always been more than a mere office building, more than a tourist attraction, more, even, than a symbol of New York City. It is, simply, the world's most famous skyscraper.

One of the reasons for the Empire State Building's fame is that the view from its observatory has attracted visitors in droves from opening day, and the view is etched in their minds. The Empire State Building is in the heart of things. You see the wall of midtown buildings and Central Park to the north, and the buildings of the financial district and the harbor to the south.

Over the years, there have been dozens of great views of New York from on high. In the late 1840s, people used to marvel at the city from the top of the city's then-tallest structure, the steeple of Trinity Church, from which pedestrians below were already being described as ants. By the twentieth century, people became accustomed to looking at the city from some of the world's tallest buildings: from the Metropolitan Life Tower, the Woolworth and Chrysler Buildings, and from the top of the World Trade Center, which was spectacular, as if you were in a helicopter that was hovering at the same spot.

Of course, the building that would have loomed large in any of the competing views was the Empire State Building itself. This is one of the city's most visible buildings, in part because it stands so majestically alone in the mountain range of New York skyscrapers. You can see it from SoHo and Little Italy, from the New Jersey Turnpike or the upper deck of the George Washington Bridge, but perhaps the best view of all is from the ramp leading to the Lincoln Tunnel on the New Jersey side of the Hudson River.

The idea for this great building germinated in 1929. The building's primary financial backer was John J. Raskob, formerly the chief financial officer of General Motors, and chairman of the National Democratic Party in 1928. That was the year the Democrats nominated New York State's Governor Al Smith as the party's standard-bearer. After Smith's loss to Republican Herbert Hoover, Smith found himself unemployed. To give Smith a job, Raskob decided to build the world's tallest building and install Smith as president. To drive home the relationship between the building itself and the building's president – the man who was both the city's most popular politician and the former governor of the Empire State – the building was named the Empire State Building.

An early plan for the Empire State Building called for an 80-story building that would have been 1,000 feet high, which was about as high as anyone thought a building could be reasonably built. Any higher, it was believed, and elevator cables were likely to collapse under their own weight.

After Smith and Raskob announced plans for their 1,000-foot-high building, Walter Chrysler, Raskob's former rival in the automobile industry, determined that he would add a stainless-steel spire to the building that he was building on Lexington Avenue between 42nd and 43rd Streets. The spire would lift the Chrysler Building to a height of 1,046 feet, and Chrysler could rightfully lay claim to the "world's tallest" title. Raskob couldn't stand still for that, so the next plan for the Empire State Building called for an 86-story building that would be 1,050 feet high. Elevators would travel to the 80th floor, where passengers would transfer to another bank of elevators serving the top six floors. Adding to Smith and Raskob's satisfaction, all 85 floors of the Empire State Building could be used for office space, unlike Chrysler's building, whose upper floors were more for show than serious use. An especial advantage to the plan was that the Empire State Building's observatory would be 150 feet higher than the observatory in the Chrysler Building, and the Empire State Building's observatory would not be enclosed, like Chrysler's, it would be an open promenade that would provide unob-

structed views, with the sky above, the city below.

Raskob and Smith decided not to stop at the 86th floor, however. Winning the laurels for "world's tallest" by a mere few feet led them to fear that somebody else would come along and do to their building what they had done to Chrysler's. So a plan was hatched that would make the building 102 stories high, lifting its height to 1,250 feet. That height would ensure the building the title of world's tallest building from 1931 until the World Trade Towers opened in 1973, but the plan was perhaps the looniest building scheme since the Tower of Babel.

The idea was to make the 200-foot-high structure atop the 86th floor a dirigible mooring mast, with regularly scheduled dirigibles arriving and departing. The planners assumed that dirigible captains would willingly brave the treacherous air currents, with all the swirling updrafts and downdrafts, and navigate their lighter-than-air crafts close enough to the building to drop a line over the side. The line would be caught, secured, winched in, and the dirigible secured. A gangplank would then be dropped from the passenger gondola to a parapet ringing the 102nd floor, and the passengers would happily walk the gangplank from the dirigible to the building, 1,250 up in the air. The developers went ahead and built the mast, but despite all the public-relations hooey, the machinery for docking dirigibles was never fully installed, and the plan was quietly scrapped. The mooring mast, however, ensured the building its title for over forty years, it gave the Empire State Building one of the most distinctive crowns that ever a skyscraper wore, and it provided another observatory where the view was said to stretch all the way to the Delaware Water Gap.

The building that was planned in the economic boom of the Twenties opened on May 1, 1931, in the financial bust of the Thirties. Management boasted that it was the "most famous address in the world," but the building only had an occupancy rate of about 23 percent when it opened. That's an inauspicious beginning when buildings that opened at 50 percent occupancy were considered off to a slow start. And the situation hardly improved. By November, 1931 – six months after opening day – the lofty Empire State Building was called "The Empty State Building."

One of the few factors that contributed to the building's solvency in its early days was the observatories. In the first year, the observatories grossed about 2 percent of the building's construction costs. Figures like that pleased Raskob, but to Al Smith the attendance was most gratifying. Smith loved the view and never tired of gazing out on his city. The city was in Smith's bones, and he would talk about the city's geography and point out every major landmark in town to anyone who would listen.

This little book has the same goal as Al Smith's great pleasure – to show you the city we call home. Enjoy the view.

John Tauranac

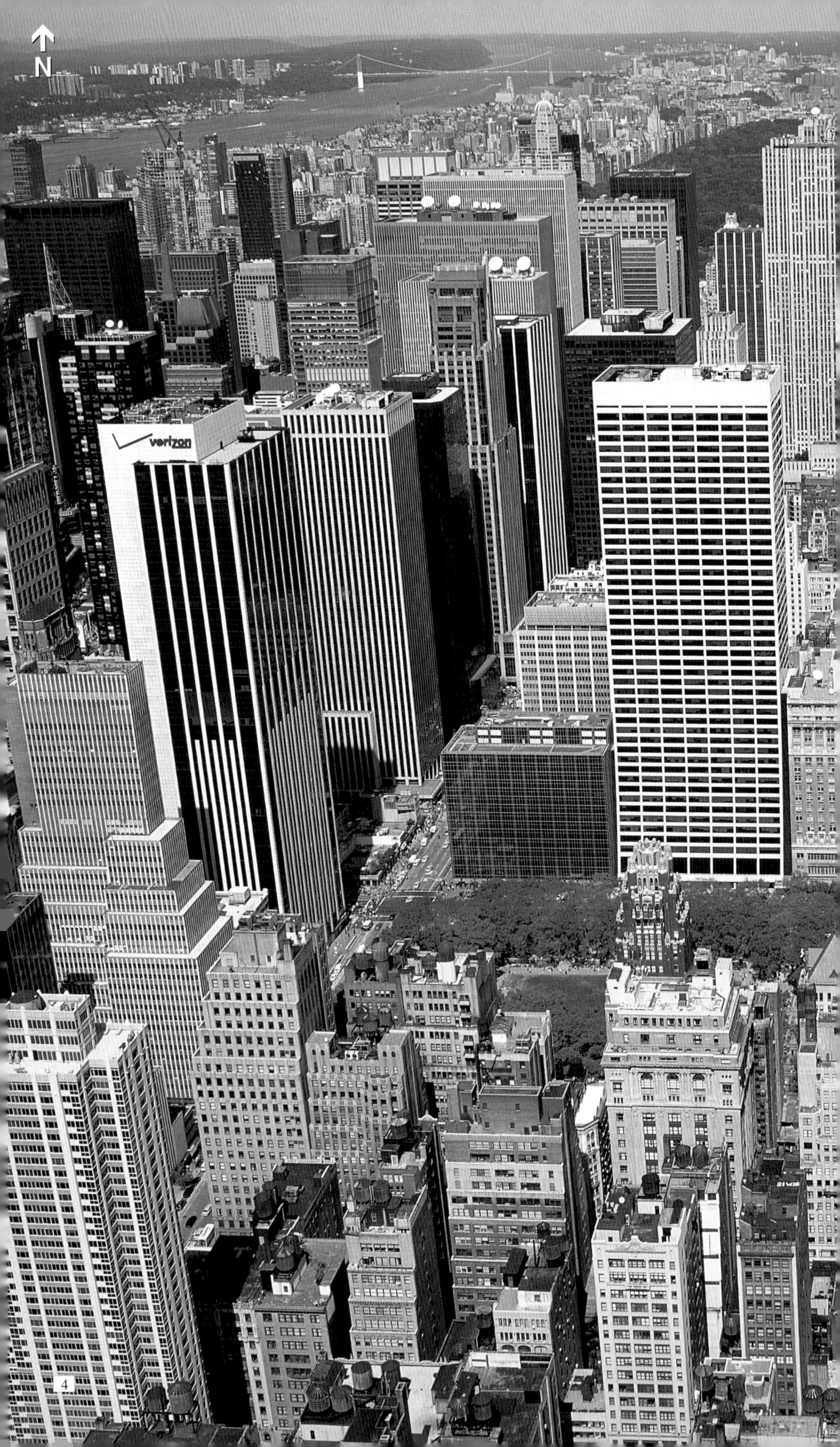
N
verizon

N

New Jersey   Fort Lee

Hudson River

AOL-Time Warner Columbus Circle (UC)

301 W 57 Apts 55 stories 1988

Random House/Park Imperial-Apts Broad-way-55 St

Paramount Plaza Broadway, 50–51 Sts 48 stories; 1971

750 Seventh Av 49th St 34 stories

Bertelsmann Building

Crowne Plaza Hotel

Millennium Broadway Hotel 52 stories

Master Apartments Riverside Dr at 103 St

Equitable Tower

Upper West Side

Little Red Lighthouse

George Washington Bridge

Riverside Church

Carnegie Hall Tower

1251 Sixth Av (Exxon) at 49th St; 54 stories

McGraw Hill-Societe« Generale 1221 Sixth Av at 48th St 51 stories; 1972 Harrison & Abramovitz

Columbia Presbyterian Hospital

Washington Heights

Har

St. John The Divine

Metropolitan Tower 57th St

CitySpire 76 stories

Credit Lyonnaise (Statues of Venus de Milo on 6 Av)

New York Hilton-

Central Park West

Central Park

GE (RC Build 30 Roc feller Pl 49 — 50 NBC stor 1933 Rockefe Center s fl buildin

AXA 1290 Sixth Av at 51st St 43 stories 1961

Time-Life Bldg

UBS Paine Webber

News Group-NY Post (Celanese Bldg) 1211 Sixth Av at 47th St 45 stories; 1973 Harrison & Abramovitz

1185 Sixth Av 46th St 42 stories 1972

1166 Sixth Av at 45th St

10 Rockefeller Pl 48th to 49th Today Show Stu

1133 Sixth Av at 43rd St 45 stories 1970 Emery Roth & Sons

Americas Tower Sixth Av at 45 St 50 stories 1992

1155 Sixth Av at 44 St 41 stories 1984 Emery Roth & Sons

Grace Building 1114 Sixth Avenue (41 West 42nd Street) 50 stories 1973 (The other building in New York with a sloping front is 9 West 57th Street; both by Skidmore, Owings & Merrill)

M

Verizon (Bell Atlantic, NYNEX New York Telephone) Sixth Avenue at 41st St 1970 Kahn & Jacobs

Hippodrome Building (named for the former Hippodrome Theater on the site)

Bryant Park Hotel (American Standard) 40 W 40 St 1924 Hood & Foulihoux

SUNY College Optome 33 W 42nd S 1912 (Aeolia Hall) Warren Wetmo

1065 Sixth Avenue aka, 111 W 40th St (Union Dime Bldg) 34 stories 1957 Kahn & Jacobs, Sydney Goldstone

HBO Building (Originally, Bryant Park Building) 1100 Sixth Avenue at 42nd Street 15 stories 1912; converted, 1984

42 Street

New York Public Librar Main Branc Fifth Avenue 40th to 42nd 1911 Carrere & Hast

Tax-payers

Sixth Avenue (Av of the Americas)

Bryant Park Studios (Originally, the Beaux Arts Studios, an artists studio building, 1901)

Bryant Park

Ant

1040 Sixth Av at 39th St 25 stories 1925 Buchman & Kahn

55 West 39th Street 16 stories

Tommy Hilfiger (Engineering Societies Building) 25 West 39th Street 12 stories

Atlas Apts SE cor, 6th Av at 38th St 48 stories 2002 Schuman Lichtenstein Claman & Efron, Archs

6 AV

42 West 39th Street 19 stories

15 West 39th St 16 stories 1925

Colony Arcade 63 W 38th St, through to 39th St

Springs Building 29 W 38th St 16 stories (Another Springs Bldg is at 104 W 40th St)

Lord & Taylor s Buyers Building 15 W 38th (In the pedin MDCCCCV

Yankee Stadium
te Office
dg - 125 St
0 Street

The Bronx
Mount Sinai Hospital

49 E 89 St Apts, at Madison Av

Upper East Side

Fifth Av

980 5 Av Apts, at 79 St

GM Building

Trump Tower 5 Av at 56 St 68 stories 1983

Four Seasons Hotel

IBM

Sony (AT&T)

520 Madison

The Bronx

Citigroup Center Lexington Av at 53rd St 59 stories; 1978 Hugh Stubbins

Trump Palace Apts 3 Av at 69 St

200 E 65 St Apts At 3 Av

Triboro Bridge Approach-Randalls Island

65 E 55 St, between Madison & Park Avs

Ritz Tower

Galleria Apts 57 St, between Park & Lexington 50 stories; 1975

Waldorf Astoria Hotel Park Av at 49 St

Solow 9 West 57th St 50 stories 1972

712 Fifth Av 56th St 52 stories 1990

717 5 Av at 56 St

International Building Fifth Av at 50th

Center

One Rockefeller Plaza 48th St (Time-Life) 1936

St. Patrick's Cathedral

Saks Fifth Avenue

500 Fifth Avenue at 42nd St 59 stories 1930 Shreve & Lamb

(In 1929, Shreve & Lamb were joined by Arthur Loomis Harmon; together, they designed the Empire State Building.)

Olympic Tower Fifth Av at 51 St 51 stories 1974

Tower 49 Between 5th & Madison 45 stories 1984

French Building

575 Fifth Av at 47th St 1985

Lefcourt National 521 Fifth Av at 43rd St 40 stories 1929 Shreve & Lamb

535 Fifth Av at 44th St 36 stories 1926 H. Craig Severance

New York Magazine (Eight million stories)

New York Palace Hotel

437 Madison Av at 49th Street

Bear Stearns 383 Madison Av, 46th—47th Sts 45 stories (With double height trading floors, much taller than the average 45-story building.) 2002 Skimore, Owings & Merrill

330 Madison Av NW cor, 42nd St 41 stories; 1963 Kahn & Jacobs

Chase World Head-quarters (Union Carbide) 270 Park 47—48 Sts 53 stories 1960 Skidmore, Owings & Merrill

277 Park 47—48 Sts 51 stories 1962 Emery Roth & Sons

Helmsley Building (NY Central) Park Av at 45th St 1929 Warren & Wetmore

Yale Club

Bank of America

Grand Central Terminal

Wn

West Street tories Midtown 927 rk & wyer

6 East 43rd St (through to 42nd St) 28 stories 1968 Emery Roth & Sons

489 Fifth Av at 41st St 34 stories 1973 Kahn & Jacobs

Quality Hotel Fifth Avenue (Journey's End)

CIBC Bldg 300 Madison Av 41st to 42nd Sts (UC)

10 E 40th St (through to 39th St) 48 stories 1929 Ludlow & Peabody

50 E 42 St SE cor Madison Av 26 stories 1917

Wonderful griffins guard this building on its upper floors

HSBC Tower (Republic Bank) 452 Fifth Avenue at 39th St 1985 29 stories Eli Attia

461 Fifth Avenue at 40th Street 26 stories 1988 Skidmore, Owings & Merrill

42 St

London Fog Building 8 West 40th St 21 stories; 1917 Starrett & Van Vleck (Goldwin Starrett was a brother of the two Starrett brothers who built the Empire State Building)

425 Fifth Avenue at 38th Street 67 stories Commercial and Residential 2003 Robert A. M. Stern

270 Madison Av at 39th St 19 stories 1925 Rouse & Goldstone

41 St

Fifth Av

445 Fifth Av at 39th St Condominium Apartments & Offices 1986 34 stories Emery Roth & Sons

Mid-Man-hattan Library

260 Madison Av at 38th St 22 stories 1952 Sylvan Bien

Lord & Taylor's Department Store ifth Avenue at 38th St 1914 Starrett & Van Vleck

420 Fifth Avenue at 37th Street Condominium Offices 1991 30 stories Brennan Geer Gorman (Site of Franklin Simon, W & J Sloane)

39 St

437 Fifth Avenue SE cor, 39th St 11 stories; 1906 C.P.H. Gilbert (GTON S is all that remains of the rooftop sign for Ovington's Silver & China Shop; see the 1997 view, P. 10)

1997
N

Photograph by Sari Goodfriend

1979
N

Photograph courtesy of Empire State Building Company LLC
managed by Helmsley-Spear, Inc

Photograph courtesy of Empire State Building Company LLC,
managed by Helmsley-Spear, Inc.

1932
N

Photograph courtesy of the Library of Congress
Prints and Photographs Division, LC-G612-T01-17580

N

Central Park

Harlem

Teresa Towers Apts (Hotel)

Harlem State Office Bldg 125 St at Powell Blvd

Jacqueline Kennedy Onassis Reservoir

110 Street
Cen
Pa

GE

Lenox Av

Powe

The rooftop observation deck offered one of the finest views in the city until it was closed in 1968. But the view from the Rainbow Room is wonderful, and you get to see the Empire State Building.

9 West 57th Street, between Fifth & Sixth Avs 50 stories 1972 Skidmore, Owings & Merrill

GE (RCA) Building
30 Rockefeller Plaza 49th to 50th Streets, west to Sixth Avenue 70 stories 850 feet; 258 m 1933 Reinhard & Hofmeister Corbett, Harrison & MacMurray Hood & Foulihoux

NBC Studios

You can't miss this sloping-front building while walking along 57th Street – a big, orangey-red *Nine* that serves the double function of signage and sculpture amiably blocks your path.

International Build
45 Rockefeller Pla
aka, 630 Fifth Aver
at 50th Street
41 stories
1935
Associated Archite

Atlas stands in fro
of this building o
Fifth Avenue.
The building hous
the frequently crow
Passport Office

AXA Financial Center
1290 Sixth Av at 51st St 43 stories 1961 Emery Roth & Sons

Rockefeller Center is the most urbane grouping of buildings in New York City. The thirteen buildings that comprise the original part of the complex were built between 1931 and 1948. Like the Empire State Building, they are sheathed in grey Indiana limestone.

AOL Time Warner (Esso)
75 Rockefeller Plaza 15 W 51st St 33 stories 1947 Carson & Lundin

Rockefeller Center

Grace Building
1114 Sixth Avenue 50 stories; 1973 Skidmore, Owings & Merrill (Site of Stern's Department Store)

This building's address is misleading. It is really 41 West 42nd Street. It could have been worse. It could have been One Grace Plaza.

One of Rockefeller Center's rooftop gardens

Ice-Skating Rink & Statue of *Prometheus*

One Rockefeller Plaza
15 W 48th Street (Originally, Time & Life Bldg) 34 stories 1937 Reinhard & Hofmeister Corbett, Harrison & MacMurray Hood & Foulihoux

10 Rockefeller Plaza (Eastern Airlines Bldg) 48th to 49th Sts The Today Show Studio occupies the SW corner of 49th Street at Rockefeller Plaza.

Jewelers & Dealers Exchange 37 West 47th Street

31 West 47th Street

47th Street Diamond District

The Exchange 15 West 47th Street

Yankee Stadium
161 St-River Av

The Bronx

Annenberg Pavilion
Mt Sinai Hospital
Fifth Av at 100th St

Taino Towers Apartments
122nd to 123rd Streets,
between Second & Third Avs, 1979

nburg
Apts
Av
th St

49 E 89th
St Apts
Madison Av
40 stories
1969

115 E 87th St Apts
Between Park &
Lexington Avs
39 stories
1973

Fifth Av

30 E 85th
St Apts
Madison Av
30 stories
1987

opolitan
eum of Art

980 Fifth Av
at 79th St
27 stories
1966

General Motors Building
Fifth to Madison Avs, 58th to 59th Sts
50 stories; 1968
Edward Durrell Stone

Upper East Side

Trump Tower
Apartments, Offices,
& Atrium
725 Fifth Av, at 56th St
68 stories
1983
Der Scutt &
Swanke Hayden Connell
(Site of Bergdorf
Goodman)

FAO Schwarz and
CBS's Early Show
are here

IBM Building
590 Madison Av,
56th to 57th Sts
43 stories; 1983
Edward Larrabee
Barnes

SONY (AT&T)
"The Chippendale
Building"
550 Madison Av,
55th to 56th Sts
37 stories; 1984
Philip Johnson
Sony Wonder
is here

712 Fifth Av
at 56th St
52 stories
1990
hn, Pederson,
Fox

Sherry-
Netherland
Hotel
Fifth Av
at 59th St
1927
Schultze
& Weaver

520 Madison Av,
53rd to 54th Sts
43 stories; 1983
Swanke, Hayden
& Connell
This building has
a pyramidal base.

Fuller
Building
Madison Av
at 57th St
Chock-a-
block with
art galleries

Henri Bendel
ccupies the
wer floors on
ifth Avenue.

Fifth Av

650 Fifth
(Pahlevi
Building)
at 52nd St
36 stories
1980
John Carl
Warnecke

717 Fifth Av
at 56th St
1958
Harrison,
Abramovitz
& Harris

Olympic Tower
Apartments, Offices & Shops
645 Fifth Avenue, at 51st Street
51 stories
1974
Skidmore, Owings & Merrill

An arcade, complete with
waterfall, leads to 52nd St
(Last site of Best & Co,
with its famous
children's department,
Lilliputian Bazaar)

Tower 49
12 East 49th Street
between Fifth
& Madison Avs
45 stories
1984
Skidmore, Owings
& Merrill

The offices of the
Major League
Baseball Players
Association
are here.

Air
Conditioning
Unit

St Patrick's
Cathedral
Fifth Avenue,
50th to 51st Sts
1878
James
Renwick, Jr.

600
th Avenue
48th Street
29 stories
1950
Carson,
Lundin
& Shaw

500 Fifth Avenue
NW corner, 42nd Street
59 stories
697 feet; 211 m
1930
Shreve & Lamb

575 Fifth Avenue, at 47th Street
40 stories
1985
Emery Roth & Sons
(Site of W & J Sloane,
Korvette's-Fifth Avenue)

u can walk
undercover
n 600 Fifth
way to the
able Tower
Seventh Av
2nd Street
Rockefeller
Center's
derground
pedestrian
arcade.

The massing and detailing are here
in a less dramatic form than
in the Empire State Building,
as if this building was a dry run
for the architects.

Saks Fifth
Avenue
49th to 50th Sts
1924
Starrett &
Van Vleck

565 Fifth Av,
at 46th St
30 stories
1993
Emery Roth
& Sons

597 Fifth Av,
between 48th & 49th
1913; Ernest Flagg
Scribner, now part of
Simon & Schuster,
has moved to Sixth Av,
but the sign remains.

CHARLES
SCRIBNER'S

Fred F. French Bldg
551 Fifth Av, at 45th St
38 stories; 1927
In the Panel:
Rising Sun = Progress
Griffins = Integrity
Beehive = Thrift & Industry

535 Fifth Av
at 44th St
36 stories
1926
H. Craig
Severance

NE

The Bronx

Hell Gate Railroad Bridge (Amtrak)

Bronx-Whitestone Bridge

Throg

Long Island Sound
Rikers Island

Citigroup Center
Lexington Av at 53rd St
59 stories; 1978
Hugh Stubbins

Triborough Bridge

New York Hospital

Bridge Tower Place Apts
1 Av at 60 St
38 stories
2000

Roosevelt Island

Astoria

Ravenswood Power Plant
"Big Allis"

Waldorf-Astoria Hotel

Abandoned helicopter landing pad

Sovereign Apts
2nd Av at 58th St
45 stories
1973

Chrysler Building
Lexington Av at 42nd St
World's tallest building, 1930, and the first one taller than the Eiffel Tower
77 stories
1,046 feet
318.8 m
William Van Alen

277 Park Av
47–48 Sts

Met Life Building
(Originally, Pan Am)
Park Avenue at 44th St
58 stories, 1961
Emery Roth,
Pietro Belluschi,
Walter Gropius
This is perhaps the New York building New Yorkers like least

780 Third Av at 48th St
(Wang Bldg)
50 stories
1984; SOM

Turtle Bay

Chanin Bldg

250 Park Av
46–47 Sts
(Postum)

450 Lexington, at 45th Street
40 stories; 1992
Skidmore, Owings & Merrill

Commerce Place
Lexington at 43rd St
31 stories
1987
Murphy/Jahn

Two Grand Central Tower

Kalikow Bldg
101 Park Av at 40th St
49 stories
1982
Eli Attia
(Site of Architects Building)

Lincoln Building
60 East 42nd St
55 stories
1930
J.E.R. Carpenter

Helmsley Building
Straddling Park Av at 45th St
Warren & Wetmore

Graybar Bldg
Lexington Av at 43rd St
31 stories; 1927
Sloan & Robertson

Bank of America
(Site of Biltmore Hotel)

Lefcourt Colonial Bldg
Madison Av at 41st St
45 stories
1929
Charles F. Moyer

100 Park Av at 40th St
36 stories
1950
Kahn & Jacobs

90 Park Av at 39th St
41 stories
1964
Emery Roth & Sons

99 Pa at 39
26 s

Grand Central Terminal

Midtown

275 Madison Av at 40th St
43 stories
1931
Kenneth Franzheim

Emery &

10 East 40th Street
(through to 39th Street)
48 stories
1929
Ludlow & Peabody

Young & Rubicam
(A true "Madison Avenue" ad agency)
285 Madison Av
NE corner, 40th St
25 stories; 1926
Rouse & Goldstone

80 Park Av A at 39th St
20 stories
1955

292 Madison Av
(Johns-Manville)
SW cor, 41 St
24 stories
1924
Ludlow & Peabody

261 Madison Av at 38th St
1954
28 stories
Sylvan Bien

270 Madison Av
NW corner, 39th St
19 stories; 1925
Rouse & Goldstone

260 Madison Av at 38th St
22 stories
1952
Sylvan Bien

260 Madison and its neighbor across the avenue at 261 are good examples of banal applications of the 1916 set-back law.

Jolly Madison Towers Hotel
Madison Av at 38th St

Madison Av

Morgan's Hotel

232 Madison Av at 37th St
16 stories
1927
Polhemus & Coffin

Polish Consul
(DeLamar Mansi
Madison at 37th
C.P.H. Gilb

38 Street

20

La Guardia (LGA) Airport

Flushing

Nassau County

Shea Stadium

Forest Hills

Citibank
44th Drive–
Jackson Av
48 stories; 1989
Skidmore, Owings
& Merrill
Long Island's
tallest building

Trump World Tower
47th St & First Av
Costas Kondylis
2001
72 stories
881 feet
The world's tallest residential building

East Elmhurst

Jackson Heights

Borough of Queens

Sunnyside

Sunnyside Rail Yards

Flushing Meadows Park
(site of '39 & '64 World's Fairs)
New York Panorama

Queensboro
(59th Street) Bridge
1909
Gustav Lindenthal

Long Island City

Pepsi-Cola Sign
1936
Artkraft Sign Co.

860 & 870
UN Plaza Apts
1966
Harrison, Abramovitz & Harris

1 & 2 UN Plaza
44th St at First Av
Hotel & Offices
1976 & 1983
Roche & Dinkeloo

UN Secretariat
First Av at 43rd St
1952; 39 stories
Harrison, Abramovitz
& an international
team of architects

Roose-velt Island

East River

Tudor City Apts
1 Av, 40–43 Sts
1925–1928
Spiderman's movie
nemesis lived in
this complex

Bel-mont Island

220 E 42nd St
(Daily News Bldg;
"Daily Planet" in
Superman movie)
Howells & Hood
1930

New York
Helmsley Hotel

Highpoint
Apts
250 E
40th St
50 stories
1988

Rooftop swimming pool

60 East
42nd St
(Socony Mobil)
Lexington
Third Avs
1955
Harrison &
Abramovitz

622 Third Av
at 40th St
39 stories
1973
Emery Roth
& Sons

600 Third Av
at 39th St
42 stories
1972
Emery Roth
& Sons

633
Third Av
at 40th St
41 stories
1962
Harrison &
Abramovitz

John Wiley
Building
Third Av
at 39th St
44 stories
1964
Emery Roth
& Sons

Paramount
Tower Apts
240 E 39th St,
bet 2nd & 3rd Avs
52 stories
1999
Costas Kondylis

355
Lexington
at 40th St
22 stories
1959
Emery Roth
& Sons

143 East
39th St Apts
(Allerton House)
1919
Arthur Loomis Harmon,
who teamed up with
Shreve & Lamb to design
the Empire State Bldg

Dryden East Apts
(Dryden Hotel–
Tel: OR9-3900)
150 East 39th St

Murray Hill
Mews Apts
Third Av between
37th & 38th Sts
37 stories
1974

Bedford Hotel
118 E
40th St

Doral
Tuscany
Hotel
120 E
39th St

Tuscany
Towers
Hotel
Lexington
Av at
39th St

Towne
House
Apts
108 E
38th St
1930
Bowden &
Russell

Carlton
Regency
Apts
Lexington Av,
NE corner,
36th St
26 stories

Park Av
39th St
stories

Lindley House
Apts
at 37th St
15 stories

Soldiers'
Sailors' &
Airmen's
Club

Penthouse
Apartment

37 St

Lexington

Tiano Hotel
6 Park Av
W corner,
38th Street

Church of
Our Saviour
Park Av at
38th Street
1959
Paul Reilly

Row Houses

Sheraton Park
Avenue Hotel
Park Av
at 37th St

Murray Hill

Union League Club
Park Av at 37th St
1931
Morris & O'Connor

23 Park
Av Apts
(Advertising
Club)
1898
McKim, Mead
& White

Houses

Morgan
Library Annex
(Stokes Mansion)

Morgan Library
36th Street, NE corner
of Madison Av
1906
McKim, Mead
& White

Morgan Court
Apts
32 stories
1985

36 St

30 Park
Av
Apts
at 36th St
19 stories

20 Park
Av
Apts
at 35th St
19 stories

21

↑ 1997
NE

Photograph by Sari Goodfriend

↑ 1960
NE

Photograph courtesy of Empire State Building Company LLC
managed by Helmsley-Spear, Inc

1953
NE

1933
NE

Forest Hills

Queens

Forest Park

Queens

Maspeth

↑E

Queens Blvd

New Calvary Cemetery
LaGuardia Community College

Long Island Expressway (LIE) I-495

Calvary Cemetery

Brooklyn-Queens Exp (Kosciuszko Bridge)

Long Island City

Citilights Apts 43 stories; 1997 Cesar Pelli

Avalon Riverview Apts 33 stories; 2002 Perkins, Eastman

Long Island Rail Road Yards

Pulaski Bridge

Brooklyn-Queens Border

Elevated tracks, Flushing Line Subway (7)

Gantry State Park

Former Pennsylvania Railroad Power Plant

Hunters Point

Horizon Apts 37th St east of First Av 44 stories; 1989 Philip Birnbaum

Queens-Midtown Tunnel Ventilation Tower

Newtown Creek

Former Daily News Printing Plant

Con Edison Waterside Electricity Generating Plant

Belmont Island

Corinthian Apts First Av between 37th & 38th Sreets 57 stories 1988 Michael Schimenti

Manhattan Place Apts First Av, 36th to 37th Sts 35 stories 1985 Philip Birnbaum

34th St Heliport & LaGuardia Water Shuttle

Rivergate Apartments First Av 34th to 35th Sts 35 stories 1985

Paramount Tower Apts 240 E 39th St, bet 2nd & 3rd Avs 52 stories 1999 Costas Kondylis

Verizon Telephone ("Ma Bell") 37th-38th Sts between 2nd & 3rd Avs

Originally, Kips Bay Brewery

37 Street

Queens-Midtown Tunnel Entrance

36 Street

First Av

St. Vartan's (St. Gabriel's) Park

35 Street

34 Street

St. Vartan Armenian Orthodox Cathedral

Murray Hill Mews Third Av, 37th to 38th Sts 37 stories 1974

Aurora Condos & Marriott Execustay 3 Av at 37 St

Parker Crescent Apts 20 stories 1963

Second Av

Second Av

200 East 36th Street Co-op Apts 19 stories 1966

Warren House Apts NW corner, Third Av at 34th St 19 stories 1961

Third Av

Soldiers' Sailors' & Airmen's Club

Carlton Regency Apts Lexington Av, NE 36th St 26 stories

Murray Hill Terrace Condo Apts Third Av at 35th St 19 stories 1963

Penthouse Apartments

35 St

36 St

35 St

Lexington Avenue

Lexington Avenue

Murray Hill

35 Park Av Apts SE cor, 36th St 18 stories

23 Park Av Apts (Originally, Robb Residence) 1898 McKim, Mead & White

35 St

10 Park Avenue Apartments (Hotel) NW corner, 34th St 26 stories 1931 Helmle, Corbett & Harrison

34 Street

Four Park Av Apartment (Vanderbilt 33rd to 34th 1912 Warren & We

30 Park Av Apts SW corner, 36th St 19 stories

20 Park Av Apts NW corner, 35th St 19 stories

Park Avenue

J F Kennedy Airport (JFK) ✈
(Idlewild Airport)

Rockaway

Atlantic Ocean

Cemetery of
the Evergreens

Jamaica Bay

Brooklyn

Williamsburg

ooklyn

Greenpoint

Waterside Apartments
East of FDR Drive, 25th to 30th Sts
North tower, 31 stories; other three, 37 stories
1974; Davis, Brody & Associates

East River

United
Nations
International
School

East
n St
cor,
Av
ts
ories
75

NYU-Bellevue Medical Center
First Av to FDR Drive
30th to 34th Sts
1950
Skidmore, Owings & Merrill

Bellevue Hospital
First Av,
27th to 29th Sts
1974

Bellevue Hospital
1908+
McKim, Mead & White

First Av

Kips Bay Plaza Apartments
First to Second Avs
30th to 33rd Streets
1960 & 1965; 20 stories
I.M. Pei

Phipps
Plaza Apts
Second Av,
26th to 29th Sts
1976

33 Street

Kips Bay

Future Apts
32nd St &
Third Av
36 stories
1995

29 Street

Laurence
Tower Apts
Third Av,
32nd to 33rd Sts
31 stories
1972

Kips Bay
Branch,
NYPL

Bentley
Apts
NW corner,
Third Av
at 30th Street
23 stories
1986

Biltmore
Plaza Apts
NW corner,
Third Av
at 29th Street
30 stories
1980

rk Avenue
to 34th Sts
es &
an Thomas
School
ories

Third Av

Windsor Court Apts
Lexington to Third Avs,
31st to 32nd Streets
31 stories
1988

Quality
East Side
Hotel
(Rutledge)
NE corner,
Lexington Av
at 30th St

ve, Lamb
mon Assocs
of the
Armory;
al eagles
rate the subway
n at 33rd Street-
Av in honor of
rmory.)

New York Design Center
200 Lexington Av,
32nd to 33rd Streets

Lexington
Avenue

32 Street

31 St

475 Park Avenue South
31st to 32nd Streets
35 stories
1970
Shreve, Lamb
& Harmon Assocs

One Park Avenue
32nd to 33rd Streets
19 stories
1926
York & Sawyer

33 Street

Two Park Avenue
32nd to 33rd Streets
28 stories
1927
Ely Jacques Kahn

N.B. Park Avenue begins at 32nd Street;
Park Avenue South ends at 32nd Street;
both were originally Fourth Avenue

33 Street

Park Av

NY
Skyports
Marina

Phipps Plaza Apartments
ES Second Av,
26th to 29th Sts
1976
Frost Assocs

Jamaica Bay

Rockaway, Queens

Borough of Brooklyn

Williamsburg

Bedford-Stuyvesant

Bro Navy

Domino Sugar Refinery

Williamsburg Bridge Main Span, 1,600 feet; 488 m 1903; Lefferts Buck

Lillian Wald & Bernard Baruch Houses

East River

Con Ed 14th Street Power Plant

Jacob Riis Houses 6th to 14th Sts

(Both Stuyvesant Town & Peter Cooper Village were Met Life projects.)

Stuyvesant Town Apts First Av to FDR Drive, 14th to 20th Sts 1947

("Gashouse District")

NY Skyports Marina

Peter Cooper Village Apts First Av to FDR Drive, 20th to 23rd Sts 1947

Veterans Administration (VA) Hospital First Av, 23rd to 25th Sts

Augustus Saint-Gaudens Playground

FDR (East River) Drive

East Midtown Apartments 23rd to 25th Sts, Second to First Avs 1972, 1974; Davis Brody & Assocs

Baruch College's Newman Library & Technology Center (1894 cable car barn)

Baruch College (Academic Com Lexington A 24th–25th S Kohn Pederse 2000

Phipps Plaza Apartments Second Av, 26th to 29th Sts 1976; Frost Assocs

2 Avenue

Fou Bu 38 at 2 16 1

Biltmore Plaza Apartments Third Avenue at 29th Street 30 stories 1980

3 Avenue

Home of Chester A. Arthur, President of the United States, 1881–1885 123 Lexington Av

Hewitt 401 P Av Sou 28th St 12 sto

St. Stephen's Church James Renwick, Jr, 1854; Patrick C Keely, 1865

419 Park Av South, SE corner, 29th St 20 stories 1927 Walter Haefli

409 Park Av South Apts, NE corner, 28th St 26 stories

Quality East Side Hotel (Rutledge) Lexington Av at 30th St

29 Street

Lexington Park Condo 137 East 30th St 18 stories; 1988

Lexington Av

Pierpont Condo Apts 111 East 30th St 19 stories; 1985

440 Park Av South at 30th St 17 stories 1913 Cross & Cross

Park Av South

443 Park Av South at 30th Street 11 stories 1910

444 Park Av South at 31st Street 12 stories (Silk Traders Bldg)

Thirty Thirty Hotel 30 E 30th St (Martha Washington)

Mad Aven SE cor 30th St 21 sto

468 Park Av South NW corner, 31st Street 16 stories 1912 (Silk Center Bldg)

460 Park Av South at 31st Street 12 stories 1910

30 St

Roger Williams Hotel 28 E 31st St, SE corner, Madison Av

Buchi &

121 Madison Av Ap NE corner, 30th S (Hubert Home Clu 1883; an early apartment house

Atlantic Ocean

New Jersey Highlands

Coney Island

Verrazano-
Narrows Bridge

ckaway, Queens

Williamsburgh
Savings Bank
1929
512 feet, 155 m
Brooklyn's
tallest building

Prospect Park

Greene

Greenwood
Cemetery

Bensonhurst

Metrotech

Downtown
Brooklyn

Brooklyn
Heights

Brooklyn Piers

DUMBO
(Down Under Manhattan
Bridge Approach)

Manhattan Bridge
Main Span, 1,470 feet; 446 m
1909; Gustav Lindenthal

Confu-
cius
Plaza
Apts

Seward Park
Houses
Grand St, 1973

Brooklyn Bridge
Main Span, 1,595 feet; 486 m
1883; John Roebling

Chinatown

kins
are
h Israel
al Center

Lower East Side

City's

Avenue A

Sara D Roosevelt Park
Chrystie St

The Bowery

Little Italy

770 Broadway
8th–9th Sts; 1904
Daniel Burnham
(Originally,
Wanamaker's)

NY
Telephone
Building

East Village

Con Ed
Tower
14th St
at Irving
Place
33 stories
1926
Warren &
Wetmore

Zeckendorf
Towers Apts

NYU Hospital
for Joint
Diseases

Park
Towers
Apts
Third Av
at 17th St
32 stories
1972

"Metronome"

rini
cal
ter

Stuyvesant
Square

2 Av

14 St
Union
Square

Elektra
Apts
(Beth Israel
Housing)
22nd St
at Third Av
32 stories

Gramercy
Park

Metropolitan
Life Tower
Madison Av
at 24th St
52 stories
700 feet,
213 m
World's tallest
building, 1909
Napoleon
LeBrun
& Sons

Baruch College
(CUNY)
Lexington Av
at 23rd St

Merchandise Mart
Madison Av,
SE corner, 26th St
42 stories
1972
Emery Roth & Sons
(Site of home of
Leonard Jerome,
father of Jenny Jerome,
mother of
Winston Churchill;
a landmark loss.)

rge
sh-
ton
tel

Metropolitan
Life Annex
Madison Av,
24th to 25th Sts
28 stories
1932
Harvey Wiley
Corbett

69th Regiment
Armory
(Site of the
Armory Show,
1913)

New York Life
Insurance Company
Madison to Park Avs,
26th to 27th Sts
33 stories
1928
Cass Gilbert
(Site of the first Madison
Square Garden)

345 Park Av South,
25th to 26th Sts
12 stories
1912

Appellate Division,
NYS Supreme Court
1900
James Brown Lord

23 Street

Mad-
ison
Squar

Goddard Bldg
11 E 26th St,
through to
27th St
21 stories
ca 1910

63 Madison Av,
27th to 28th Streets
16 stories
1961
(New York Life is the
sole office tenant.)

Madison
Square Bldg
15 E 26th St,
through to
27th St
20 stories
1912

Gift Bldg
225 Fifth Av,
26th to
27th Sts

Emmet Bldg
95 Madison Av,
SE corner, 29th St
16 stories; 1913
Barney & Colt

Madison Belvedere Apts
10 East 29th St,
between Fifth &
Madison Avs
50 stories
1999
Schuman Lichtenstein
Claman & Efron

245 Fifth Av,
SE corner, 28th St
26 stories
1927

Madison Av

iamie
yflower
Bldg
Madison,
29th St
stories
1916

Carlton Hotel
(Seville)
88 Madison Av,
SW corner, 29 St
Circa, 1905

Home
Furnishings
Textile Bldg
261 Fifth Av,
SE corner, 29th St
26 stories
1928
Buchman
& Kahn

dison Av

102 Madison Av,
NW corner,
29th Street
12 stories
1917

35

5 Av

28 St

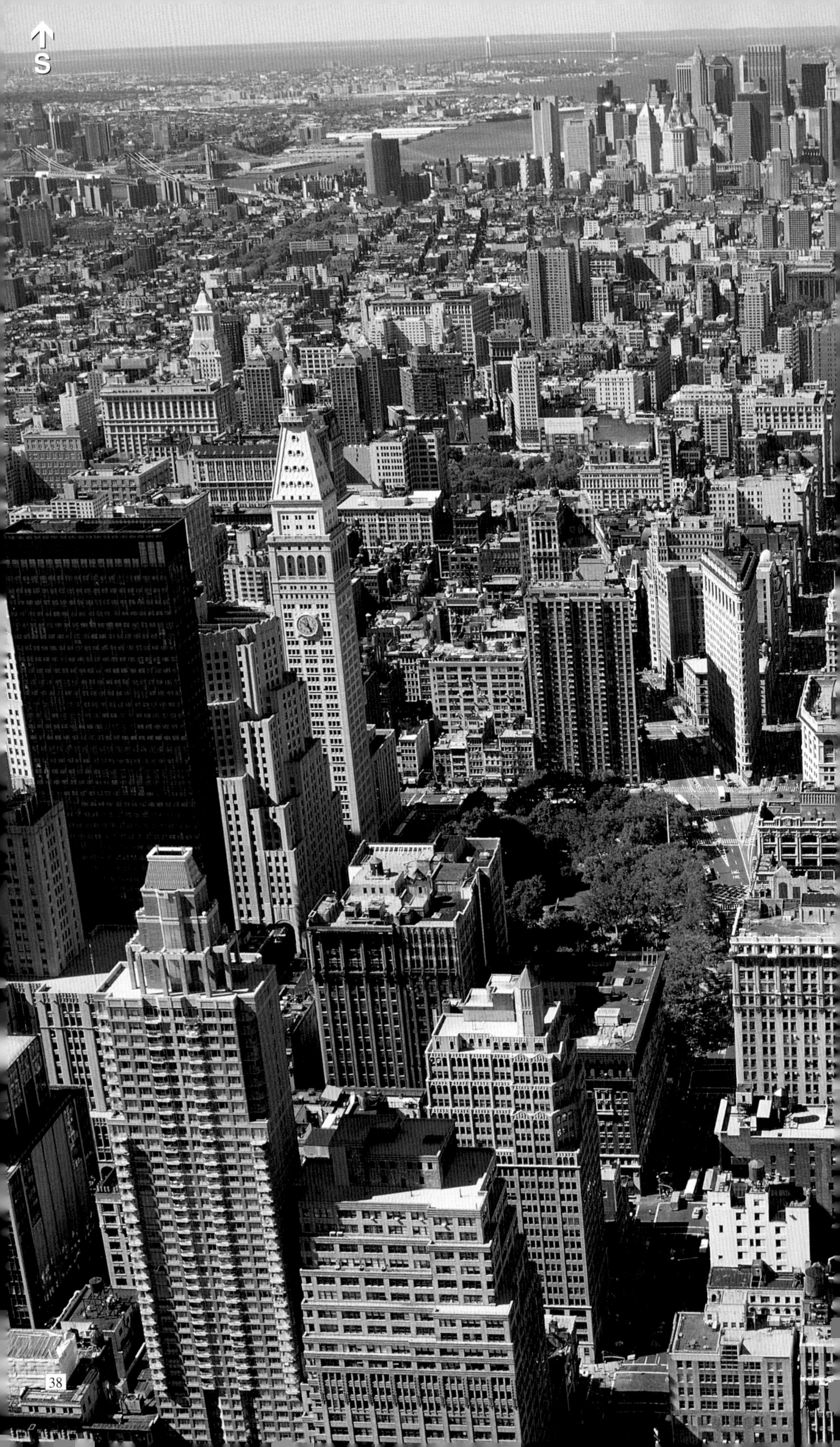
S

N
S

Atlantic Ocean

New Jersey Highlands

Verrazano-Narrows Bridge
World's longest suspension
bridge, 1964

70 Pine Street

Morgan

Woolw Build

Chase Man-hattan

HSBC

Prospect Park

Greenwood Cemetery

Brooklyn Bridge
World's longest
suspension bridge, 1883

NY Tele-phone

Municipal Bldg

Financial District

15 Park Row

Downtown Brooklyn

Brooklyn Heights

Manhattan Bridge

Bush Terminal

Confucius Plaza Apts

East River

US Courthouse (Pearl St)

US Courthouse (Foley Sq)

Univers Village A

Canal St

Detention Center ("The Tombs")

Lower East Side

S D Roosevelt Park

Bowery

Mott St

Chinatown

Little Italy

Georgetown Plaza Apts 8th St 31 stories

New York University

Bobst Library

St. Mark's in the Bowery

Astor Place

40 Fifth SW corner, 11th (The disappear Judge Cra lived he

Con Ed Tower 1926 Warren & Wetmore

Zeckendorf Towers 14th to 15th Sts, Union Sq to Irving Pl

One Union Square South &"Metronome"

Broadway

14 Street

122 Fifth Av (Broadcast studio for WQXR, 96.3 FM, which transmits from the Empire State Building's antenna.)

Union Square (Green Market)

Merchandise Mart SE corner, Madison Avenue at 26th Street 42 stories 1972 Emery Roth & Sons

Metropolitan Life Tower Madison Av at 24th St World's tallest building, 1909 52 stories 700 feet; 213 meters Napoleon LeBrun & Sons

Madison Green Apts Broadway, between 23rd & 24th Sts 32 stories 1983 Philip Birnbaum

Flatiron Building 21 stories; 1902 Daniel Burnham (Tall, yes, but not the world's tallest building in 1902.)(Sohme

170

Fifth

Toy Center Fifth Av to 24th S

Metropolitan Life Annex Between Madison & Park Avs, 24th to 25th Sts 1932 Harvey Wiley Corbett

Madison Avenue

23 Street

Madison Square

Broadway

23 Street

New York Life nsurance Company Madison to Park Avs, 26th to 27th Sts 33 stories 1928 Cass Gilbert

Goddard Bldg 11 East 26th St, through to 27th St 21 stories ca 1910

212 Fifth & 1134 Broa at 26th Str 21 stories;

Madison Belvedere Apts 10 East 29th Street, between Fifth and Madison Avs 50 stories 1999 Shuman Lichtenstein Claman & Efron

Madison Square Bldg 15 East 26th St, through to 27th St 20 stories 1912

Gift Bldg 225 Fifth Av, 26th to 27th Sts 12 Stories 1907 Francis H. Kimball

The Marketce 27th Street bet Fifth Av & Broa 21 stories 1914

245 Fifth Av SE corner, 28th Street 26 stories 1927

63 Madison Av 27th to 28th Sts 16 stories 1961

Home Furnishings Textile Bldg 261 Fifth Av, SE corner, 29th St 26 stories 1928 Buchman & Kahn

Fifth Avenue

downtown
S

E — crosstown — W

Madison Av

uptown
N

260 Fifth Av, at 29th Street 12 stories

The City passed a zoning law in 1916 that said that buildings could rise straight up a certain multiple of the width of the street they faced; above that height, setbacks were required, as shown in 245 and 261 Fifth Avenue. Towers were allowed to rise as high as technologically feasible on 25 percent of the plot. It explains the form of the Empire State Building.

Marble Collegiate Church

Site of the World Trade Towers
World's tallest buildings, 1973
110 stories; 1,350 feet; 411 m
Destroyed in a terrorist attack,
September 11, 2001

Battery Park City/
World Financial Center

NY Telephone

101 Barclay

Independence Plaza Apts

Smith Barney (Travelers)

TriBeCa Pointe Apts

SoHo Grand

TriBeCa

Staten Island

Kill Van Kull

NY Harbor

Ellis Island

Statue of Liberty

State Dept (Passport office) 380 Hudson St at Houston St

Saatchi & Saatchi 375 Hudson St at Houston St

Bayonne

Jersey Central RR Terminal

Holland Tunnel Ventilating Shaft 1927

New Jersey

Elizabeth

Exchange Place

Harborside Financial Center

Hudson River

Pier 40 Garage at Houston St

SoHo

NYU Law

Atrium Apts (Mills House No. 1) Bleecker St

29 Washington Sq (Eleanor Roosevelt's pied à terre)

MacDougal

435 Hudson St at Morton St

Archive Apts Greenwich & Christopher Sts

Greenwich Village

St. Vincent's Hospital

Jefferson Market Sixth Av at 9th St

NY Foundling Hospital

620 Sixth Av 18th to 19th Sts Bed & Bath & Beyond, Filene's, etc (Siegel-Cooper, 1896–1914)

Salvation Army, 14th St

625 Sixth Av, 18th to 19th Sts Today's Man, etc. (Yesterday's B. Altman, 1877–1906)

Former home of Barneys, with its Husky Boys' Shop

"Bell Telephone" is inscribed over the 18th St entrance of this telephone building.

675 Sixth Av, 21st to 22nd Sts Barnes & Noble (Adams Dry Goods Store, 1900–1915)

Photography District

Ladies' Mile

Seventh Av

Bozell 40 W 23rd St (Stern's Dry Goods Store, 1870's–1920's)

Masonic Hall 71 W 23rd St, through to 24th 19 stories 1912

Arlington Hotel 18 W 25th St

36 W 25th St 16 stories

Show Place 40 W 25th St

24 St

Capitol at Chelsea Apts 55 W 26th St, NE corner Sixth Av 39 stories 2002 Costas Kondylis

Chelsea Tower 100 West 26th St Apts 35 stories 2002

Center th way h St

St. James Bldg 1133 Broadway SW corner, 26th Street 16 stories 1896 Bruce Price (Emily Post's father)

1155 Broadway SW corner, 27th St

Broadway

26 St

Sixth Avenue

Johnston Bldg 1170 Broadway, at 28th St 1903 12 stories; 170 feet to the top of the gilded dome Schickel & Ditmars

Baudouine Bldg (With a great rooftop temple) Broadway at 28th St 1896 Alfred Zucker

Salz Bldg (loft building) 44 W 28th St, east of Sixth Av 16 stories

Breslin Apts (Hotel) SE corner, Broadway at 29th St 1903; Clinton & Russell

Wallach Building Broadway at 29th St 10 stories; 1929 Louis Shampon

28 Street

Photograph by Sari Goodfriend

1986
S

1937
S

Photograph courtesy of Empire State Building LLC,
managed by Helmsley-Spear, Inc.

Photograph courtesy of the New York City Municipal Archives

S / N

New Jersey

American
International Bldg
(Cities Service)
70 Pine Street
Third tallest building in
the world, 1931
67 stories
950 feet; 288 m
Clinton & Russell

Raritan Ba

Approach to
Verrazano-Narrows
Bridge

Staten Island

Staten Island

20 Exchange Place
at William St
(City Bank Farmers Trust)
57 stories
760 feet; 231 m
1931
Cross & Cross

New York
Harbor

55 Water St
at Old Slip
53 stories
Emery Roth
& Sons
With 3.68 million
square feet, this was
the world's largest
private office
building, 1973;
Zip Code, 10041

J. P. Morgan Bldg
60 Wall Street
(Pine St façade)
47 stories
1988
Kevin Roch,
John Dinkeloo

This building has an
enchanting, trellis-lined
ground-level arcade
and entrance
to the subway.

Civic Fame,
Adolph A.
Weinman

Financial Square
32 Old Slip,
at South Street
36 stories
1987
Edward Durrell
Stone Assocs

Barclay's Bank
75 Wall Street,
between Pearl
& Water Sts
36 stories
1986
Welton Becket

80 Pine Street/
110 Maiden Lane
38 stories
1960
Emery Roth
& Sons

Jacob K Ja
Federal Office B
between Lafayett
& Broad
Duane & Worth
41 sto
Erecte
two stages
in two st
on Lafayette, 1
on Broadway,
Alfred Easton P
Kahn & Jac
Eggers & Hig

Royal Globe
Insurance Bldg
150 William St,
at Fulton St
19 stories
1927
Starrett &
Van Vleck

U.S. Courthouse,
Southern District
40 Centre Street
at Foley Square
38 stories
1936
Cass Gilbert

Inside traders
Ivan Boesky &
Michael Milken,
and the 1993
World Trade
Center bombers
were tried here.

Municipal Building
1 Centre Street,
straddling Chambers St
25 stories
1914
McKim, Mead & White

When people say they are
getting married at City Hall,
this is usually the building
they mean.

150 Nassau St,
at Spruce St
23 stories; 1896
Robert H. Robertson
(Originally, the
American Tract
Society, publisher
of religious tracts.)

The scu
Richard Se
controversial "T
Arc" stood on
plaza in fro
this buildi
the 1990s. T
is accountin
public taste afte

Court Square Bldg
2 Lafayette St,
between Duane &
Reade Streets
21 stories; 1927
Buchman & Kahn

346 Broadway,
between Broadway &
Lafayette St at Leonard St
(New York Life Insurance Co
12 stories, 1896

Civic Center

80 Lafayette Street,
at White Street
18 stories
1915

(Tenants include the
Legal Aid Society,
and the City's Dept
of Social Services and
Dept of Transportation)

Family Court
Lafayette Street
at Franklin Street

Ma
Plaz
Bro
at W
25

Broadway

New Jersey

Raritan Bay

Staten Island

New York
Harbor

40 Wall Street
Trump Building
(Bank of Manhattan)
World's tallest building, 1929
70 stories
927 feet; 282.5 meters
H. Craig Severance,
Yasuo Matsui

One Liberty Plaza,
Broadway at Liberty St
(U.S. Steel)
53 stories; 1973
Skidmore,
Owings & Merrill
(Site of the
Singer Tower
world's tallest
building, 1908)

One Chase Manhattan Plaza
tween Liberty & Pine Streets,
Nassau & William Streets
60 stories
1961
Skidmore, Owings
& Merrill

David Rockefeller built this
ffice building in the hope of
vigorating Lower Manhattan.
succeeded, and then some.

inancial District

15 Broad St,
at Exchange Place
(Morgan Guaranty)
43 stories
1928
Trowbridge &
Livingston

HSBC
(Marine Midland)
140 Broadway
at Liberty St
52 stories
1967
Skidmore,
Owings &
Merrill

The street-level view
on Broadway is enlivened
by Isamu Noguchi's Cube,
whose orange color and
qurky angles are the perfect
foil for the restrained,
rectlinear building.

Woolworth
Building
233 Broadway
at Park Row
World's tallest
building, 1913
55 stories
792 feet;
240 m
Cass Gilbert

One
Wall St,
at Broadway
Bank of
New York
(Irving
Trust)
52 stories
1931

Transportation
Building
225 Broadway,
at Barclay St

ral agencies
de the Court
ernational
(Customs
), Corps of
eers,
erce
rtment,
al Bureau of
tigation (FBI),
al Trade
mission (FTC),
rtment of
e,

222 Broadway,
between
Fulton & Ann Sts
(Western Electric)
31 stories
1961

American Telephone &
Telegraph Long Lines Bldg
Church Street, between
Thomas & Worth Streets
1974
John Carl Warnecke

The design of this building
makes sense when you
realize that it was built to
withstand nuclear attack.
The question remains,
who would there be to call?

Federal Office
Building (EPA)
290 Broadway,
between Duane &
Reade Streets
(Site of the African
Burial Ground)
32 stories
1994
Hellmuth, Obata
& Kassabaum

Park Row
Building
World's tallest
building, 1899
32 stories
390 feet, 118 m
15 Park Row,
between Ann &
Beekman Streets
Robert H.
Robertson

TriBeCa
Tower
Apts
Duane St
at Broadway
53 stories
1990

Tower Gallery
te for Art &
Resources)
oadway,
nard St

401

401 Broadway
at Walker St
26 stories

City Hall
Park

The vertical
stripes reflect
elevator shafts

This area is now called TriBeCa,
which is a City Planning Commission
acronym for the Triangle Below Canal (Street).
SoHo is another acronym: South of Houston (Street).

SW

SW

New Jersey

Liberty Science Center

Bayonne

Newark Bay

I-78 Newark Bay Bridge

Newark Airport (EWR) ✈

Jersey City

Jersey City Medical Center

Jersey City

Holland Tunnel Entrance

I-78

Harborside Financial Center

Newport Center/ Pavonia

Hudson Place

Hoboken Ferry Terminal

Memphis Apts 140 Charles St, between Greenwich & Washington Sts

Holland Tunnel Ventilating Shaft 1927

Westbeth Artists' Apartments (Bell Labs) 155 Bank St Washington to West Sts

Hudson (North) River

West St

NYC Sanitation Dept

346 W 17 St (National Maritime Union)

Robert F House (NYCH 16th to 19

Greenwich Village

Washington St

St. Peter s Church

Warehouse, Eighth to Ninth Avs, 15th to 16th Streets (Union Inland Terminal No. 1) 16 stories, 2.3 million sq ft 1932

Chelsea

Original Home of Barneys, with its Husky Boys' Shop

Verizon (New York Telephone; Bell Telephone) 206 W 18th St 19 stories

Kensington House Apts SW corner, 7 Av at 20 St 14 stories

Chelsea Hotel 222 West 23rd St 12 stories; 1884 (Past guests include Brendan Behan, Thomas Wolfe & Tennessee Williams)

300 V 23rd St 19 sto

7 AV

Westminster Apts 7 Av, 19—20 Sts 16 stories 2001

Chelsea Savoy Hotel 1997

Carteret Apts 208 W 23 St 18 stories 1926

Seventh Av

275 Seventh Av (loft building) 25th to 26th Sts 26 stories 1928

Former McBurney YMCA 23 St, between 7 & 8 Avs (McBurney Y now on 14 St)

7 Av

Chelsea Tower 100 West 26th St Apts 35 stories 2002

"Indus Buildi 150 28th 18 sto

Capitol at Chelsea Apts 55 W 26 St, NE cor, 6 Av 39 stories 2002 Costas Kondylis

777 6 Av Apts, between 26 & 27 Sts 2001

Chelsea Arts Building 134 W 26th St

104 W 27th St 12 stories A beauty of a neo-classical commercial loft building.

109 W 27th St 12 stories

TADA Youth Theater 120 W 28th St

26 St

6 Avenue

27 Street

Flower District

Salz Bldg (loft building) 44 W 28th St, east of Sixth Av 16 stories

Sixth Avenue (Av of the Americas)

28 St

104 W 29th St 12 stories

Wallach Building 1195 Broadway NE cor, 29th St 10 stories

46 W 29th St 14 stories

These buildings show the scale of the average building on Sixth Avenue in the 1890s.

29 Street

Newark

Pulaski Skyway

Union City

Hoboken

Elysian Park
(The Elysian Fields,
where the first game
of baseball was said
to be played according
to the "New York" rules.)

Hackensack
River

New Jersey Turnpike / -95

Stevens Institute
of Technology

Sinatra Drive

Todd Shipyards

Golf
Driving
Range

Chelsea Piers Sports &
Entertainment Complex

Yacht &
Dining
Cruises

Basketball
City

hattan
i Storage
rchants
igerating Co)
n St at 10th Av

11 Av

General
Theological
Seminary

London Terrace Apts
(Named for the "terrace" rowhouses
these buildings replaced)
23rd to 24th Streets,
Ninth to Tenth Avs,
1930

12 Avenue

Chelsea-Elliott Houses
(NYCHA)
Ninth to Tenth Avs,
25th to 27th Streets,

10 Avenue

Church of the
Holy Apostles
9 Av at 28 St
1848
Minard Lafever

322
Eighth Av
Loft Bldg
NE corner,
26th St
20 stories
1925

Penn Station South Apartments
(ILGWU Co-ops)
Eighth to Ninth Avs, 23rd to 29th Streets
1962

th Avenue

Fashion Institute
of Technology

Eighth Avenue

29 St

Tower
enth Av
orner,
St
ories

Seventh
Avenue Bldg
(Loft Building)
28th to 29th Streets
22 stories
1920
Schwartz & Gross

7 Penn Plaza
370 Seventh Av,
at 31st St
(Holmes Bldg)
17 stories
1931

This hotel's
original name was
"Governor Clinton"

144 W 30th St
(Loft Building)
20 stories

Southgate Tower
Suite Hotel
Seventh Avenue,
SE corner, 31st Street
31 stories
1929
Murgatroyd & Ogden

11 Penn Plaza
Matthew Bender Bldg
(Equitable Society,
Montgomery Ward)
393 Seventh Avenue,
31st to 32nd Streets
23 stories
1925
Starrett & Van Vleck

130 W 30th St
Loft Building
18 stories

Greeley Arcade
132 W 31st St,
through to 30th St
18 stories
1925
George & Edward Blum

St. Francis
of Assisi Church

Taylor Business
Institute

30 St

Greeley Sq Bldg
875 6 Av
NW cor, 31 St
26 stories
1927
Gronenberg & Leuchtag

Originally, Gimbel's
Warehouse

57

Passaic

Newark Bay

↑
W

Hoboken

Starrett-Lehigh Bldg
11th to 12th Avs,
26th to 27th Sts
22 stories; 1931
2 million square feet
Russell & Walter Cory,
Yatsuo Matsui
(Martha Stewart has
space here)

Church of the
Holy Apostles
Ninth Av at 28th St
1848
Minard Lafever

10 Avenue

Chelsea
Park

French Apts
330 W 30th St
(Originally, the
French Hospital)

Penn Station
South Apartments
(ILGWU Co-ops)
Eighth to Ninth Avs
1962

29 Street

Originally,
the power
plant for
Pennsylvania
Station

7 Penn Plaza
30th to 31st Sts
(Originally, the
Holmes Bldg,
370 Seventh Av)
17 stories
1931

Southgate Tower
Suite Hotel
(Originally, Hotel
Governor Clinton)
Seventh Avenue at 31st St
31 stories; 1929
Murgatroyd & Ogden

Govs. Al Smith and
Franklin D. Roosevelt
both attended the
banquet celebrating
the opening of the
Gov. Clinton Hotel.

25 Street

28 Street

30 Street

Morgan
Processing &
Distribution Center
US Postal Service

Claytor-Scannell
Amtrak-LIRR
Control Center

31 Street

9 Av

11 Penn Plaza
Matthew Bender Bldg
Between 32nd & 33rd Streets
(Originally, the Equitable
Society Bldg;
then Montgomery Ward;
393 Seventh Avenue)
23 stories; 1925
Starrett & Van Vleck

Hudson (North) River

30th Street
Heliport

Liberty
Helicopter
Tours

12 Avenue

11 Avenue

Abandoned Rail Tracks

Long Island Rail Road
West Side Storage Yard

450 West 33rd St
10th Av, 31st to 33rd Sts
16 stories; 1970
Davis, Brody
(The Daily News
and WNET-TV
are tenants.)

10 Av

Farley Building
General Post Office
NY, NY 10001
("Neither Rain Nor Snow....")
Eighth Avenue, 31st to 33rd Sts
1913; 1935
McKim, Mead & White

33 Street

Two Penn Plaza
(400 Seventh Av)
Between 31st & 33rd Sts
1968; 31 stories
Charles Luckman
(Pennsylvania Station, below;
Madison Square Garden, behind)

This office-entertainment complex
replaced the late, great Penn Station

Madison Square
Garden :
Site of the
2004 National
Republican
Convention,
home to the
NY Knicks,
Liberty, &
Rangers, and
to Barnum &
Bailey

Pennsylvania Hotel
(Statler Hilton, Penta)
401 Seventh Av,
between 32nd & 33rd Sts
30 stories; 2,200 guest rooms
1918
McKim, Mead & White

This hotel still has the same
telephone number made famous
by Glenn Miller,
PEnnsylvania 6-5000

33 Street

7 Avenue
(Fashion Av)

33 Street

St. Francis of Assisi
Church & Monastery
135 West 31st Street,
through to 32nd Street

Manhattan Mall
(Originally, Gimbel's)
On Greeley Square,
Broadway between
32nd to 33rd Streets

Children's
Wear
Center
100 W 33rd St

Internatio
Childre
Apparel Cen
131 W
33rd

Union City

Secaucus

Reservoir

Lincoln Harbor
Complex
1987

Ramp
Linco
Tunn

1 Penn Plaza
Seventh Av,
33rd to 34th S
55 stories; 197
Kahn & Jacob

New Jersey

Giants Stadium

Brendan Byrne Arena

Meadowlands

Hackensack River

NJ Turnpike I-95

eehawken

I-495

West New York

Aaron Burr killed Alexander Hamilton here in a duel in 1804.

Lincoln Tunnel Ventilating Shaft 1937 Othmar Ammann & Ralph Smillie

Port Imperial

Circle Line Sightseeing Cruises Pier 83 42nd St

United Parcel Service

Jacob K. Javits Convention Center Eleventh Av, th to 39th Streets 1986; I. M. Pei

Auto Violation Tow Pound Pier 76

NY Waterway Ferry Pier 78, 38th St

Lincoln Tunnel Ventilating Shaft 12 Avenue

World Yacht Cruises Pier 81 41st St

Mike Quill Bus Depot NYCT

River Place Apts 41 stories 2000 42 Street

Consulate General of China (Sheraton)

Riverbank West Apts 44 stories 1988

2 Av

1 Av

Haddon Hall Apts 20 stories

NEW YORKER 36 Street

Remco 501 10 Av

Mercedes Benz

St. Raphael Church

Hunter College MFA

0 Av

34 Street

GHI 441 9 Av

Hotel New Yorker Eighth Av at 34th St 43 stories 525 feet; 159 m 1930 Sugarman & Berger

505 8th Av, at 35th St (Originally, the Hoover Bldg) 25 stories 1926

10 Avenue

Lincoln Tunnel Entrance

38 Street

Ramp to Port Authority Bus Term

9 Av

5 Penn Plaza (461 8th Av) Cable News Network (CNN)

519 8th Av, SW corner, 36th St 25 stories 1926

Herogel Building 325 W 36th St 19 stories 1926 Blum & Blum

Arcade Building 520 8th Av, 36th to 37th Sts 27 stories; 1926 Schwartz & Gross

265 West 37th St, NE corner, 8th Av Almost a twin of the neighboring Arcade Bldg

8 Av

Nelson Tower 450 7th Av, at 34th St 46 stories 560 feet; 170 m 1931

Garment District

Garment Center Realty Bldg 36th to 37th Streets 24 stories; 1.5 million sq ft 1921 Walter M. Mason

Pennsylvania Building 225 W 34th St 2 stories; 1925 hwartz & Gross

H. Craig Severance This building is eight feet shorter than Cincinnati's tallest building, the Carew Tower.

36 Street

462 Seventh Av, at 35th St 23 stories 1925

York Apts (Hotel) Seventh Av at 36th St

34 Street

MACYS

Arsenal Bldg 463 7th Av, at 35th St 21 stories; 1925 Ely Jacques Kahn (The name of this loft building commemorates the arsenal on this site that was defended against looters during the Civil War Draft Riots in July, 1863.)

Fashion Atrium Seventh Av at 36th St (Mills House No. 3) 15 stories Ernest Flagg

7 Avenue (Fashion Av)

Air itioning ant

34 Street

Macy's World's largest department store, 1902 Herald Square Store, DeLemos & Cordes; Westward extensions, 1924–1931, Robert D. Kohn

35 Street

36 Street

Johnson Bldg Broadway, 35th to 36th Streets 12 stories

1997
W

Ca. 1960

Photograph courtesy of Empire State Building Company LLC, managed by Helmsley-Spear, Inc.

Meadowlands

New Jersey

Hackensack

Hackensack River

West New York

Riviera Towers

Weehawken

Hudson (North) Ri

Port Imperial Marina

Riverbank West Apts 42nd St, between 10th & 11th Avs 44 stories 1988

Strand Apts 43rd St at 10th Av 42 stories 1990

Carnival Cruise Liner

Circle Line Sightseeing Cruises Pier 83 42nd St

Intrepid (Aircraft Carrier) Sea-Air-Space Museum

Passenger Ship Terminal Piers 88 – 92

DeWitt Clinton Park

River Place Apts 41 stories 2000 Costas Kondylis

UPS

Consulate General of China (Sheraton)

Victory Apts 10th Av, 41st– 42nd Sts 47 stories 2002 SCLE, Archs

New Gotham Apts

Manhattan Plaza Apts 42nd to 43rd Sts, 9th to 10th Avs 45 & 46 stories 1977 David Todd

330 W 42nd St (McGraw-Hill Bldg) Between 8th & 9th Avs 35 stories 1931 Raymond Hood

Ivy Tower 41 stories 2002 SCLE, Archs

Clinto (Hell's Kitc

42 Street

11 Avenue

420 W 42nd St, at Dyer St (between 9 & 10 Avs) 2001 Hardy Holzman Pfeiffer

10 Avenue

St. Raphael Church

40 Street

Dyer St

Holy Cross (Father Duffy church)

Lincoln Tunnel Entrance

Ramp to Port Authority Bus Terminal

Port Authority Bus Term.

Port Autho Bus Term 8th Av, to 42nd

39 Street

Baer Bldg 575 Eighth Av, NW corner, 38th St 23 stories 1926

The Navarre 7th Avenue at 38th St 44 stories 1930 Sugarman & Berger

8 Avenue

Arcade Bldg 36th to 37th Streets 27 stories 1926 Schwartz & Gross

265 W 37th St 22 stories Lofts & Apts

530 Seventh Av, at 39th St 30 stories

Fashion District

Fashion Center Bldg 525 Seventh Av, NE corner, 38th S

Garment Center Realty Bldg 498 7th Avenue, 36th to 37th Streets 24 stories 1.5 million sq. ft. 1921 Walter M. Mason

501 Seventh Av, at 37th St 18 stories 1924 Ely Jacques Kahn

Lefcourt State Bldg 1375 Broadway NW corner, 37th Street 26 stories 1927 Ely Jacques Kahn

462 Seventh Av NW corner, 35th St 23 stories 1925

Fashion Tower Seventh Av at 37th St 22 stories 1925

York Apts (Hotel) 7th Av at 36th St

Arsenal Bldg 463 7th Av, NE corner, 35th St 21 stories 1925 Ely Jacques Kahn

Armion Bldg 7th Av at 36th Street 16 stories

Fashion Atrium 7th Av at 36th St (Mills House No. 3) 15 stories Ernest Flagg

141 W 36th St 22 stories

Lefcourt Marlboro Bldg 1359 Broadway NW corner, 36th Street 22 stories 1925 George & Edward Blum

1 Broad SE 37th 16 sto

37 St

Macy's Department Store is one of the city's major benefactors, with its gifts of fireworks on July 4th and the parade on Thanksgiving, which is affectionately called "The Macy's Day" Parade. A different kind of gift is "Miracle on 34th Street."

Johnson Bldg 1333 Broadway, 35th to 36th Sts

Herald Square Bldg Sixth Av to Broadway, 35th to 36th Streets 25 stories 1929 Clinton & Russell (Site of the Herald Building, the newspaper that gave rise to the name Herald Square)

New Jersey

Cliffside Park

Worldwide Plaza Offices
8th Av, 49th to 50th Sts
49 stories; 1988
Skidmore, Owings & Merrill
(Site of second Madison
Square Garden)

3 Lincoln
Center Apts
66th St
60 stories
1991

Fort Lee

Lincoln-
Center

Galaxy
Apts

Con Edison
(Originally, IRT Subway
Power Plant; McKim,
Mead & White; 1904)

Joe Dimaggio
(West Side)
Highway

West End Tower Apts
62nd to 63rd Sts
39 stories; 1995

Trump Place
Atop the West
Side rail yards
68th–71st Sts

Paramount Plaza
Broadway at 50th
48 stories; 1971

on Tower Apts
h Av at 54th
39 stories

AT&T
(Switching
Center)
10th Av
at 53rd St

Bertelsmann
Broadway
at 45th St
44 stories
1986
SOM

555 West
57th St,
at 11th Av

Marriott Marquis
Broadway,
45th to 46th Sts
1985
John Portman

47 Tenth
Av Apts
at 50th
38
stories

AT&T
50th St,
between 9th
& 10th Avs

CBS
News

World-
wide
Plaza
Apts
35
stories
1988

1 Astor Plaza
(Grant)
Broadway,
44th to 45th Sts
54 stories; 1972
Kahn & Jacobs
(Site of
Astor Hotel)

Condé Nast
4 Times Square
1476 Broadway,
NE cor. 42nd St
1999
Fox & Fowle

Millenium
Broadway Hotel
145 W 44th St

Westin New
York Hotel
SE cor,
43 St-8 Av
46 Stories
2002
Arquitec-
tonica

Graphic
Communication
Arts High School

Ernst & Young
5 Times Sq
WS Broadway,
41st–42nd Sts
37 stories
2002
Kohn Pedersen Fox

Reuters
3 Times Sq
WS Broadway,
42nd–43rd Sts
2001
Fox & Fowle

1501
Broadway
(Paramount
Theater)

Times
Square

Verizon
(Bell Atlantic,
NYNEX,
New York
Telephone,
Ma Bell, etc.)
1095 Sixth Avenue
41st–42nd Streets
41 stories
1970
Kahn & Jacobs

World Apparel
Center
1411 Broadway,
39th to 40th Sts
40 stories
1968
(Site of the
Metropolitan
Opera House,
1883–1963)

1441
Broadway
SW cor,
41 St
34 stories
1929
Ely Jacques
Kahn

7 Times Sq
Broadway to 7th Av,
41st–42nd Sts
48 stories
2004 (UC)
Skidmore
Owings
&
Merrill

1450
Broadway,
at 41st St
42 stories
1931
Ely
Jacques
Kahn

1065
Sixth Avenue
(111 West
40th Street)
34 stories
1957
Kahn & Jacobs,
Sydney Goldstone

Broadway
o 39th Sts
stories
1950
& Jacobs

Marriott
Courtyard Hotel
Nobutaka Ashihara
Assocs; 1999

Springs Bldg
104 W 40th St
20 stories; 1962
Harrison,
Abramovitz
& Harris

1400 Broadway
NE corner, 38th Street
35 stories
This was billed as the
world's largest dress building
when it opened in 1930.
Ely Jacques Kahn

1040
Sixth
Avenue
NE corner,
39th Street
25 stories
1925
Buchman
& Kahn

Lefcourt
Normandie
Building
SE corner,
Broadway
at 38th St
25 stories

Atlas Apts
SE cor,
6th Av at 38th St
48 stories
2002
Schuman Lichtenstein
Claman & Efron, Archs

1001 Sixth Av
NE corner,
37th Street
23 stories

Millinery Center
Synagogue

Sixth Av,
7th Street
tories

38 Street

Sixth Avenue
(Av of the Americas)

Vogue Apts
990 Sixth Av
36th to 37th Streets
25 stories
1987

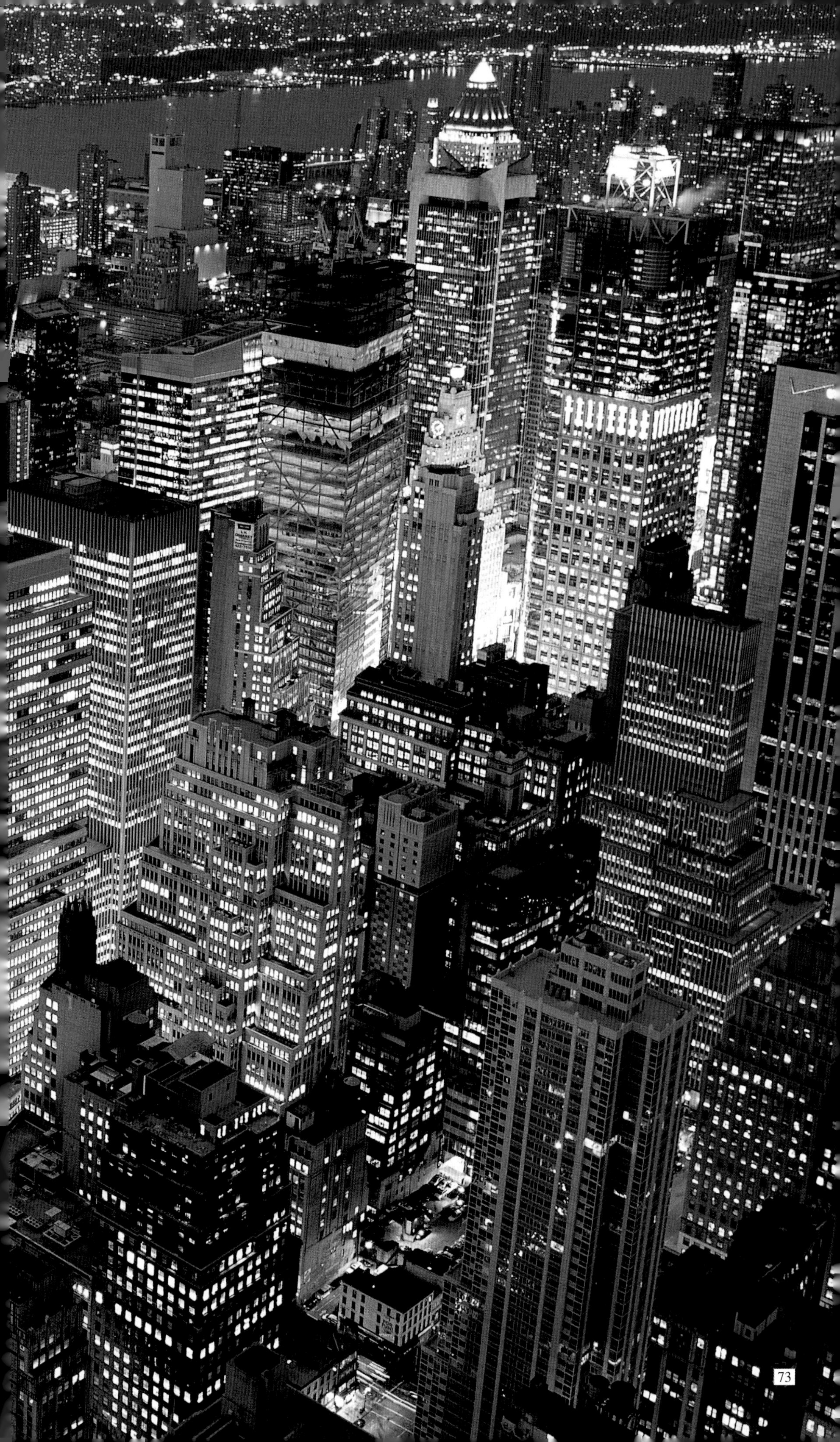

MACY'S

1950
NW

In the 1890s, this stretch of Fifth Avenue was lined with millionaires' mansions, with lesser homes – rowhouses – lining the side streets. By 1931, the majority of buildings you see here were already built, and there was only one mansion still used as a private dwelling on this stretch of Fifth. It was home to a recluse named Ella Wendel, who was the last of the neighborhood Astors, the family that had started the neighborhood development in the 1850s with a pair of mansions on the site of the Empire State Building.

When the Empire State Building opened in 1931, this stretch of Fifth Avenue was lined with department and specialty stores that included B. Altman, Best & Co., Gorham Silver, Tiffany's, Franklin Simon, and Lord & Taylor, which is the only major store still on Fifth in the neighborhood. Thirty-fourth Street had Oppenheim Collins and McCreery's. Then as now, the side streets between Fifth and Sixth Avenues have been filled with loft buildings occupied by tenants who specialize in some aspect of the garment industry.

N

Atlas Apts
66 W
38 St

Colony Arcade
63 W 38th St,
through to 39th

Lord & Taylor's
Buyers Bldg
15 W 38th St
MDCCCCVIII

Lord & Taylor
Fifth Av
at 38th St
1914

420 Fifth
Avenue,
at 37th St
1991
30 stories
(Site of
Franklin
Simon)

425 Fifth Av
Apartments

260 Madison
at 38th St

417 Fifth Avenue
1915, Buchman & Fox
(An early home
of Bonwit Teller)

38 St

Springs Bldg
29 W 38th St

15 W
37th St

411 Fifth Avenue
11 stories
1915
Warren & Wetmore
(Grand Central's architect)

Millinery
Towers
49 W 37th St
17 stories

39 W
37th St
18 stories

7 W
37th St

38 St

Fifth Av

Vogue
Apts
990 Sixth,
36th to
37th Sts
25 stories
1987

Garment District

37 St

409 Fifth Avenue
SE corner, 37th Street
McKim, Mead & White
(Tiffany & Co.,
1906–1940)

53 W
36th St

45 W
36th St

25 to 35 W 36th St

15 W
36th St

7 W
36th St

Textiles

16 to 28 W 36th St

36 Street

36 St

Fifth Avenue

70 W 36 St
1940
16 stories

390 Fifth Av,
SW corner, 36th St
McKim, Mead
& White; 1906
(Originally,
Gorham Silver;
still bearing its
great cornice)

Metro Hotel
(Collingwood)
12 stories

29 W 35th St
12 stories
1911

372 Fifth Av,
NW corner, 35th St
(Originally, Best & Co.,
with Lilliputian Bazaar)

33 W 34 St,
through to 35 St
(Franklin Simon,
Oppenheim Collins)

Comfort
Inn
(Gregorian
Hotel)

7 West 34th St,
through to 35th
Limited Express
(McCreery's,
Ohrbach's)

The unmistakable shape
of the shadow cast by the
dirigible mooring mast and antenna
atop the Empire State Building.

35 Street

City University
Graduate Center
(Originally, B. Altman)